If This Fumbled Kiss Ever Ends, I'm Going to Write Her a Poem

100 Senryu

G.C. McRae

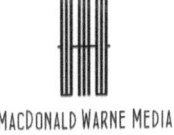

MacDonald Warne Media

If This Fumbled Kiss Ever Ends, I'm Going to Write Her a Poem
words and images by G.C. McRae

Published by MacDonald Warne Media
Copyright© G.C. McRae 2023
All Rights Reserved

ISBN: 978-1-7776351-0-7

Poetry, Illustrated

This book is produced only in eco-friendly POD and eBook editions.

No part of this book may be reproduced or transmitted in any form or by any means, electronic or mechanical, including photocopying, recording or by any information storage and retrieval system without express written permission from the author/publisher.

Visit us at: gcmcrae.com

for Nora

CONTENTS

The Red-Rumpers	1
That New Baby Smell	23
Lawnchair Bagatelles	45
Wet Collies	67

1.

The Red-Rumpers

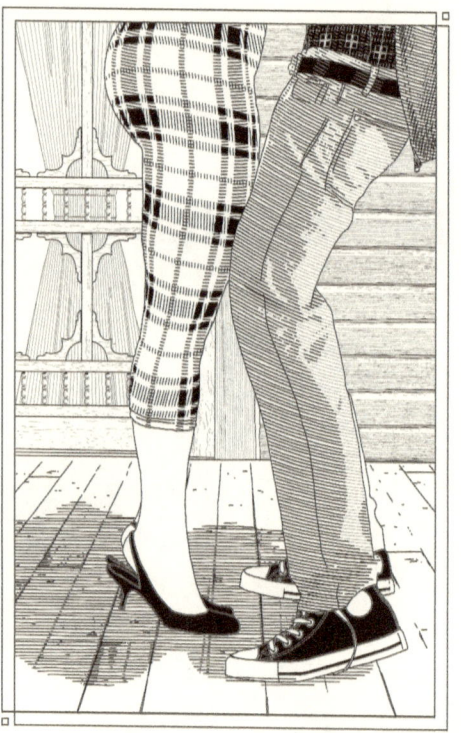

if this fumbled kiss
ever ends, I'm going to
write her a poem

I move my fingers
thus...cupping, smoothing, spreading
and back again, slow

                        the darkness crouches
                        leaps for the moon and devours
                        it with thunderclouds

the conversation
into the wee hours, so deep
we forgot to speak

bet those arms could pick
me up and throw me into
the valentine aisle

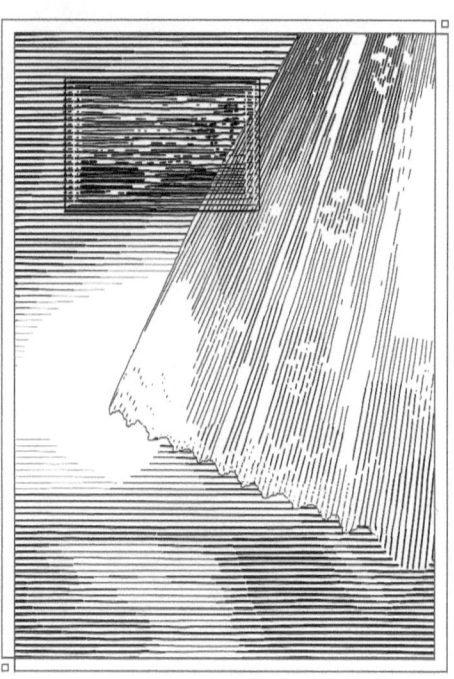

some days I think I
could be pushed past ecstasy
with a little breeze

petals in the snow
proving the ideal time for
everything is now

at night, wind through the
trees: the official soundtrack
of mortality

every weather is
perfect on the other side
of a window pane

                              I will never know;
                              had only enough cash and
                              courage for one date

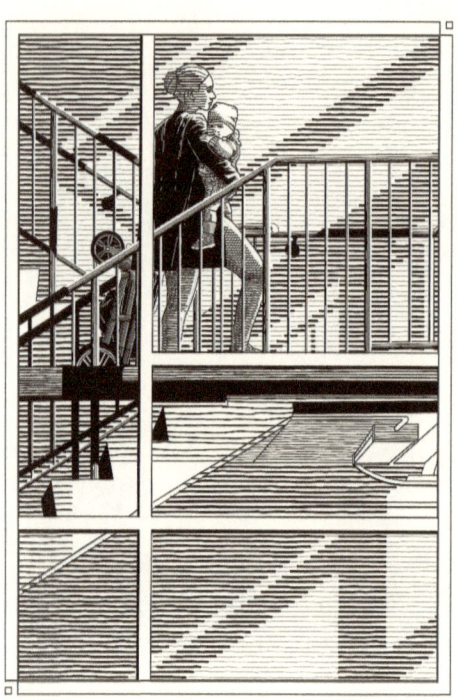

the morning stairwell
valley-lilied in the wake
of the working girls

cubicle snug, plays
solitaire, eats like you would
load a pellet gun

                        she pauses typing;
                        everything looks real in the
                        5:40 sunlight

bath done, she's again
the calm one, the prodigy
the hairy goddess

late, she still has time
to Rorschach the eyelash from
the bathroom mirror

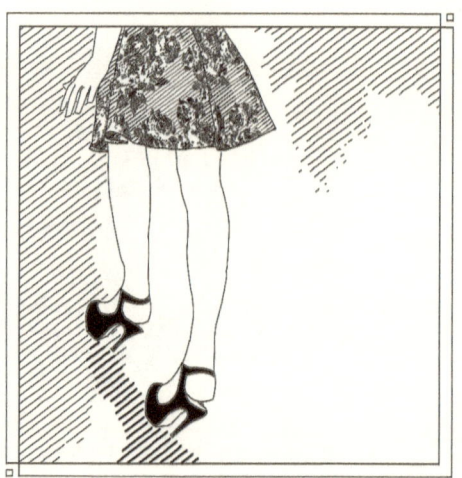

new high shoes, makeup
perfect, best dress in the world
and each step a risk

Saturday night, the
club is full of beta males
red rumps and yearning

festival ticket
was for a front row cot in
the medical tent

no matter what you
do on nightshift, you can't help
feeling like an orc

saturated drunks
squeeze out of the pub like earth
worms after a rain

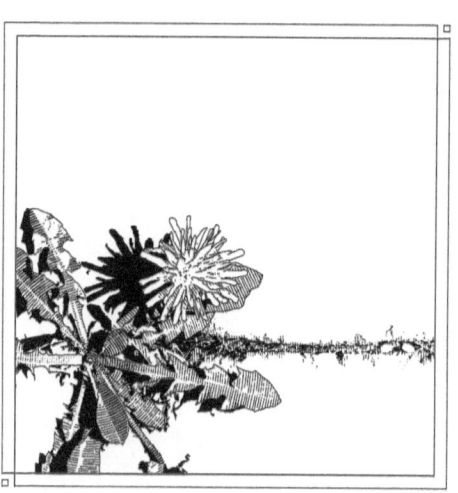

the lone weed between
the buildings has enticed the
only patch of sun

weekend alchemist
transmogrifying paycheques
into liquid gold

morning, the magpie
persnicks the ochre vomit
on the tavern wall

to watch for the bus
a thumbnail sketch of quack grass
in the window frost

I'm not sure, but I
think my body's laughing at
me behind my back

2.

That New Baby Smell

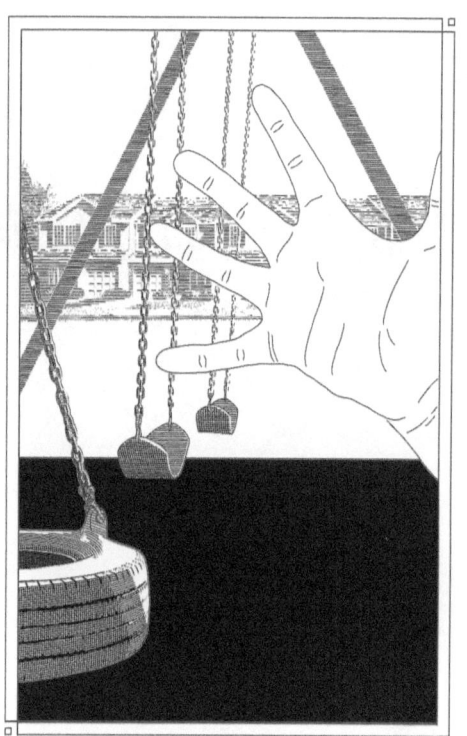

her whole little arm
slaps air at my face; I can
count to five, she says

the rain-wet wipers
swish the confetti aside
in two tearful lines

my little snowman
is standing up on the porch
eating the carrot

dreading laundry day
she cannot bear to wash out
that new baby smell

she picks up the paw
print from the snow, breaks it like
a cookie and laughs

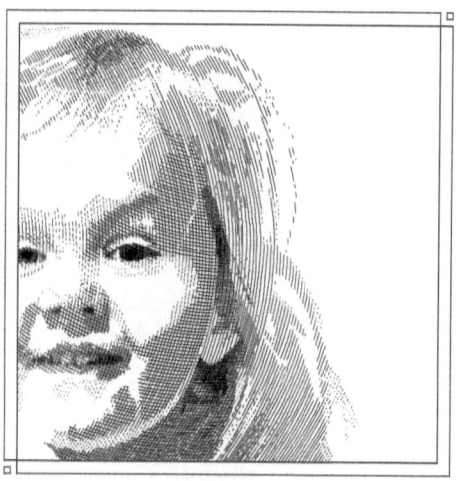

small girls with doll clothes
and a plan: the real reason
kittens are born blind

under the blankets
in their own secret language
snowflake twins giggle

          home to his daughter
          the grime deeper than his skin
          hugs with his elbows

most of the winter
the wee bear sleeps in the dark
cave of his navel

                        the dying, the rich,
                        even the squirming kid, all
                        salute the eclipse

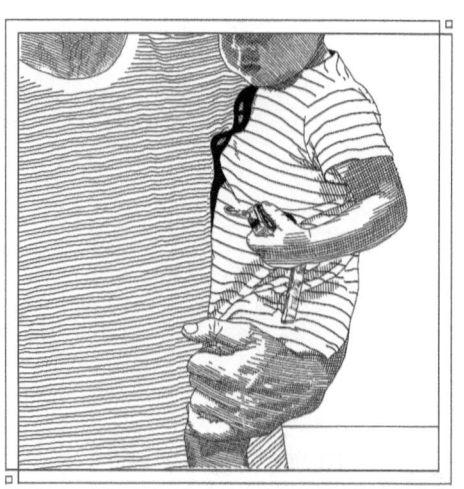

seems so long ago
just walking around with a
boy-sized hole in me

playing with his young
son, cheek to sidewalk, thinking
now it feels like spring

the ball game stops cold
to watch a daddy longlegs
eating an apple

is that the sweet smell
of spring's exuberance or
someone's clothes dryer?

guilt cage: frosted eyes
of splatted crab apples watch
through my son's window

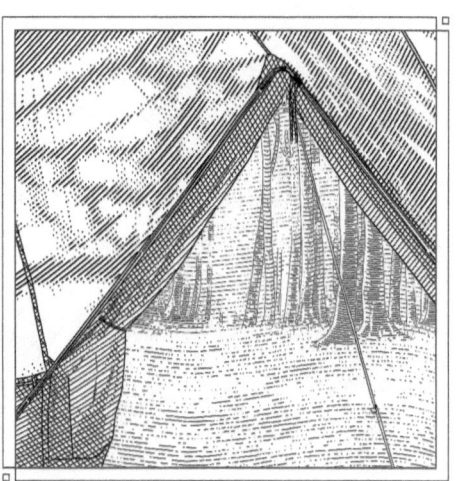

camping, my girl says,
how can I see the bears if
you zip up the tent?

old enough to know
the taste of every twig and
green leaf on his street

                          the robin perches
                          by us dummies picnicking,
                          stamps his three small toes

she tumbles, gets up,
flings the sand out of her hair
and shouts, I'm still 'it'

two reasons for not
wanting to get out of bed:
love, and losing it

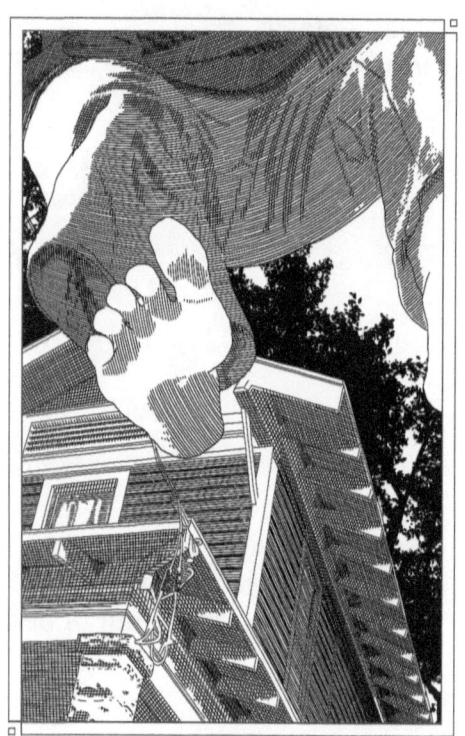

the rain must have stopped;
the neighbor kid is outside
hopscotching earthworms

careful, she's bearish
if she is roused too early
from her screen-lit den

                              at the bus stop, the
                              kid with the cracked phone sneers a
                              the fiddlehead gusts

it's so still and cold
his merry Christmas hovers
like a cartoon ghost

                        choked up at my desk
                        because the elevator
                        just smelled like crayons

3.
Lawn Chair Bagatelles

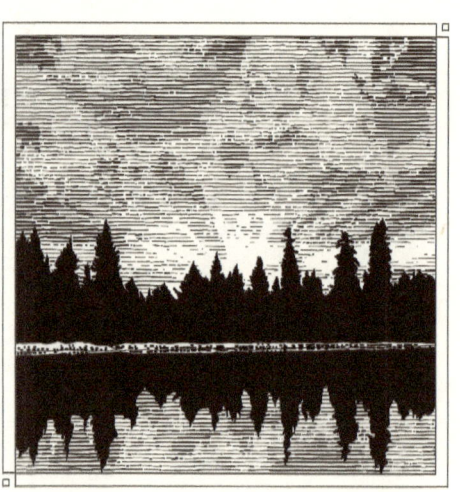

one cricket reviews
the night's performance, just as
the house lights go up

the first sign of spring:
mule deer cavorting in the
snow, thawing for crows

the river parts us
into those who jog its banks
and those who sleep them

clattering maple
hoists a jolly Safeway bag
over the wind's spoils

squirrel, sounding like
she's holding a rolling pin
castigates blue jay

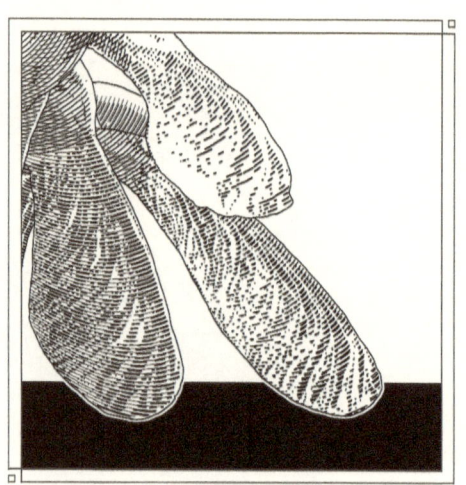

maple leaves and seeds
or some tale of mice and ears
Icarussing down

magpie's jumbled nest:
bottle caps, dog nuggets and
vole fur welcome mat

by feline soccer
rules, a whole mouse shall never
foul the field of play

the April sun carves
a collie turd pieta
from the marbled snow

the bird has Elvis
hair, wonders at the ice with
eyes like loose buttons

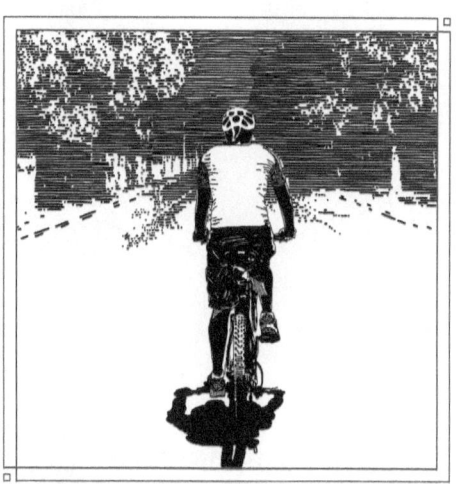

summer, 3:00 a.m.
the wake of the bicycle
smells like a snowbank

I wonder how the
rose feels about my aunt's spit
and hankie treatment

the full history
of my meandering tastes
written in belt holes

poised with the kettle
she thinks better of it and
leaves the ants alone

                                damn, before she died
                                I should have got her to knit
                                me a grandmother

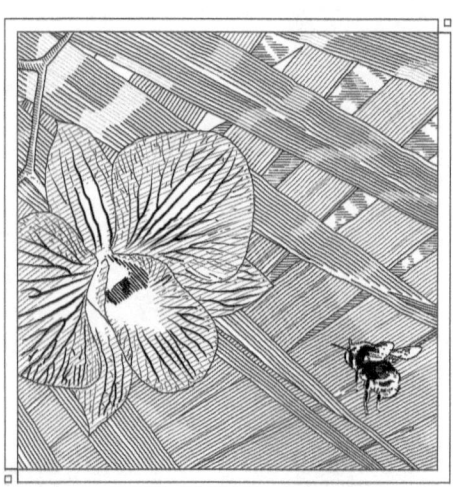

sated, orchid airs
its velvet tongue, bee returns
for dusty seconds

after the setter
trees her, she loses her last
eye to a magpie

since we each breathe in
specks of rotted Will Shakespeare
I named my dog Spot

deer, the carrot greens,
gophers, from the bottom up
and mice, the root tops

whoever carved that
heart and initials loved a
girl but hated trees

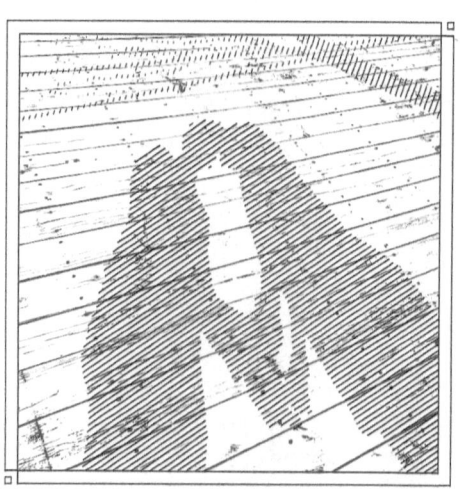

decades at this, still
dense as oak about love, yet
felled, limbed, bucked and split

this chinook valley
tangible Brahms requiem,
choir, spit valves and all

cursing a moss flap
he weeds the lawn in a touque
and shorts, shirt untucked

these raked leaves, a great
big pile of every other
age I've ever been

                        the trees are out in
                        their snowsuits, standing very
                        still to feed the birds

4.

Wet Collies

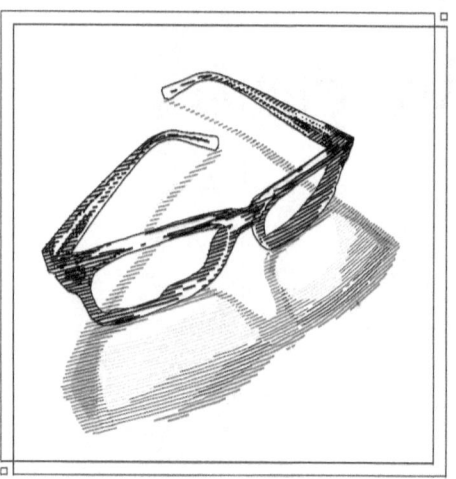

beauty's in the eye
of the beholder who knows
where his glasses are

elbowing the wind
you would think she had been hooked
by a vaudeville cane

                        the house looks haunted
                        in autumn, but in springtime
                        ivy whisks the ghosts

all those big snowflakes
spraying slow from the streetlights
worth the sleepless night

                              she spends so much time
                              at church even the gargoyles
                              are praying for her

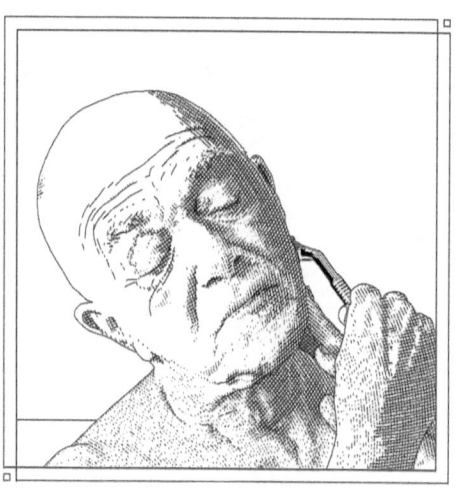

half a damn life spent
mowing lawn; hurts to think I'll
be it when I'm gone

too old for doubt, she
dresses by the fluff of the
birds at the feeder

night comes, the house pulls
up a warm shadow, coughs a
guest and rolls over

coronation plate
complexion, hidden somewhere
between her laugh lines

not afraid to die,
she's just afraid she might die
embarrassingly

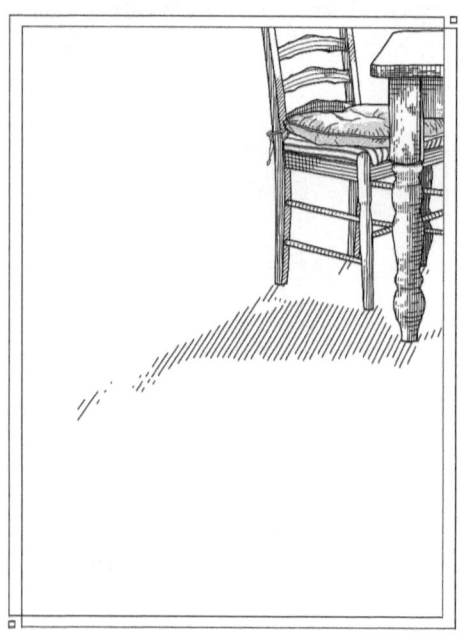

insignificant
sitting in this chair worn by
so much history

born in this kitchen;
of course, it has to smell like
salmon at the end

after her fall, she
was too weak to make the steps
and returned inside

the air is tepid,
unmoving, a sensory
overload chamber

clear after the rain
the house smells of carrot tops
wet collie, regret

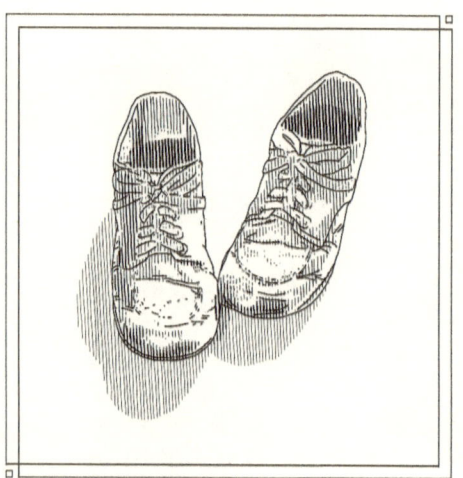

they went through her things
found the shoes the bronzer bronzed
and those he couldn't

mid-funeral blink:
mine's the only memory
of me as a child

artfully thorough
knowing it's the last time I'll
ever paint this fence

four hundred million
breaths in a life, and not a
bad one in the bunch

we miss you sweet birds
you'd hate it here anyway
there's no place to land

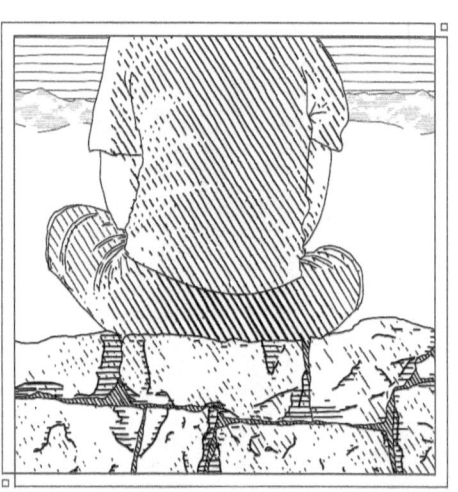

so disappointing
to travel six thousand miles
and find yourself there

what will they recall?
last man with his name used to
come in to buy tools

I move my fingers
thus... knowing the story of
each embellishment

no one cares about
your arrival time, if all
your sails were hoisted

tales of summer on
each leaf, the tree arranges
its winter reading

*With heartfelt thanks to
Greig Rasmussen
who shaped the first draft of this collection
and set me on the course that led us all here.
Thank you, Greig. Look what you did!*

www.ingramcontent.com/pod-product-compliance
Lightning Source LLC
Chambersburg PA
CBHW031447210526
45464CB00005B/2356